KATHARINE
HEPBURN
Once Said . . .

Also by **Susan Crimp**

Touched by a Saint: Personal Encounters with Mother Teresa

Iron Rose: The Story of Rose Fitzgerald Kennedy and Her Dynasty

Caroline and Stephanie: The Lives of the Princesses of Monaco

KATHARINE HEPBURN

Once Said . . .

GREAT LINES TO LIVE BY

Collected by Susan Crimp

HarperEntertainment

An Imprint of HarperCollins*Publishers*

KATHARINE HEPBURN ONCE SAID . . . Copyright © 2003 by Susan Crimp. All rights reserved. Printed in the United States of America. No part of this book may be used or reproduced in any manner whatsoever without written permission except in the case of brief quotations embodied in critical articles and reviews. For information address HarperCollins Publishers Inc., 10 East 53rd Street, New York, NY 10022.

HarperCollins books may be purchased for educational, business, or sales promotional use. For information please write: Special Markets Department, HarperCollins Publishers Inc., 10 East 53rd Street, New York, NY 10022.

FIRST EDITION

Designed by Betty Lew

Printed on acid-free paper

Library of Congress Cataloging-in-Publication Data has been applied for.

ISBN 0-06-058172-7

03 04 05 06 07 ❖/RRD 10 9 8 7 6 5 4 3 2 1

In gratitude for the great joy

Kate gave us here on earth

"Oh, we're going to talk about me, are we? Oh, goody!"

—*THE PHILADELPHIA STORY,* 1940

Contents

Introduction . . . . *xiii*

On Self *1*

On Life *25*

On Love and Marriage *57*

On Career and Acting *77*

On Fashion *95*

On Confidence *107*

On Spencer Tracy *119*

On Other Leading Men *129*

On Aging Gracefully *139*

On Death *149*

Filmography *153*

Acknowledgments *155*

Source Notes *157*

Introduction

To fully comprehend the enormous impact Katharine Hepburn had on the world, upon her death on June 29, 2003, more than twenty years since she made her last motion picture, even the president of the United States of America stopped to pay homage. "Katharine Hepburn delighted audiences with her unique talents for more than six decades," said George W. Bush. "She will be remembered as one of the nation's artistic treasures."

Indeed, Hepburn was a star quite unlike any other, and even though she spent the last years of her life in relative seclusion, we all felt a little better knowing she was still around. Hepburn stood for another era. A time when Hollywood represented grace, elegance, and style. Sadly, we will never see her likes again. Yet we can reflect on the tremendous contribution she made to the twentieth century.

A four-time Oscar winner and bestselling author, Katharine Hepburn was one of the greatest dramatic talents the world has ever seen. She was larger than life both on- and offscreen, and Hepburn's legendary performances, coupled with her fierce intelligence, sharp wit, and uncanny wisdom, propelled her to iconic status and won her a permanent place in all our hearts. Hepburn was not just an American original but also a universal one. Nicknamed "Kate the Great," she completely lived up to the moniker. A woman who, through the many roles she played and the way she lived, became not only a role model to millions of women but also a shining and articulate example of how, even in Hollywood, amazing talent, perseverance, and impeccable character can prevail. She has left a legacy that inspired many of today's A-list actresses.

Hepburn also played her characters with so much ease that one began to wonder whether there wasn't a little piece of her in each of them. She was equally individual offscreen, frequently refusing inappropriate casting, publicity, and the usual superficialities of show business. Hepburn did what she wanted, on her own terms, and most of the time, to everyone's amazement, her way paid off.

During her career, Hepburn worked with many of the greatest stars in the world, including Cary Grant, Burt Lancaster, John Wayne, Humphrey Bogart, Henry Fonda, Elizabeth Taylor, and Sir Laurence Olivier. She also proved one did not have to be British and recite Shakespeare to be a master at the craft of acting. Yet Hepburn's career, during which she received twelve Oscar nominations, was not without its ups and downs. During the 1930s, several of her films flopped and she was dubbed "box-office poison." She was also called cantankerous by some of her fellow professionals. After an electrifying and Oscar-winning performance in *The Lion in Winter,* it emerged she had actually hit her costar, Peter O'Toole, during the film's production. Hepburn later remarked. "It improved his performance." In all, she appeared in fifty films, and in 1999, the American Film Institute ranked her the greatest actress of all time.

Throughout her life Katharine Hepburn said many different things. Some of her lines were written for her, while others are original Hepburnisms. This book is intended to preserve some of Hepburn's most memorable lines both on-screen and off. It is a little tribute to a legend. A truly remarkable woman who touched each of our lives in so many different ways. A keepsake that will enable us to treasure the memory of her forever.

—S.C.

On Self

"No one does it alone. Your success belongs to the people who are holding you up. I can only say that I am the product of adorable people. I've been so lucky, just lucky."

"Mother and Dad were perfect parents. They brought us up with a feeling of freedom. There were no rules. There were simple certain things which we did—and certain things which we didn't do because they would hurt others."

"I'm bossy—I'm adorable."

"I don't care how afraid I may be inside—I do what I think I should."

———■———

"Everyone thought I was bold and fearless and even arrogant. But inside I was quaking."

"My greatest strength . . . common sense. I'm really a standard brand—like Campbell's soup or Baker's chocolate."

———■———

"I was fortunate enough to be born with a set of characteristics that were in public vogue."

"I'm not good at public life."

"I think that if you're lucky enough to belong to an era that you live in, in a very strong way, as I did, then you're lucky. So I'm lucky."

———■———

"I have the capacity to accept the inevitable. The terrible things that happen . . . the losses of people you adore . . . terrific disappointments. I say, 'Well, that's not going to change,' and on you go!"

"I'm always working on something because I have to be busy."

———■———

"I get the nominations because I'm always playing freaks. The awards generally go to the sad, dramatic freaks."

"I think to myself, 'What would it be like if they didn't say, "Oh, hello Kate."' That would be funny, but I've never known that."

"I like every damned thing about the place. Palms and brown hills and boulevards and geraniums six feet tall, and flowers running riot everywhere, and the grand roads and the golfing, and the picture people and even the work, grinding as it is. I like it! Why in the hell shouldn't I?"

—ON HOLLYWOOD

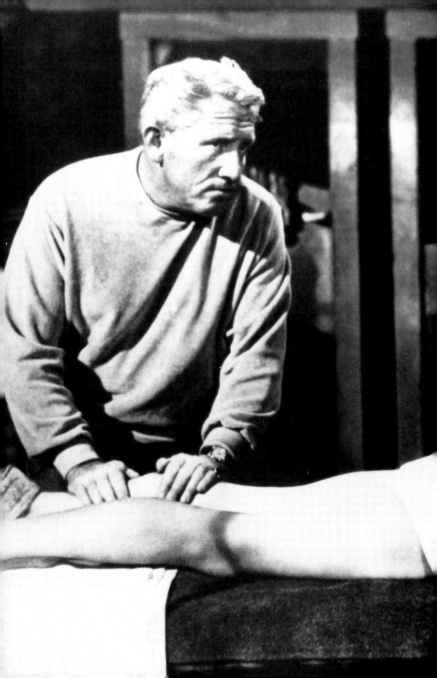

"You see, it's never you against the whole world . . .
Just you against yourself!"

—*PAT AND MIKE*, 1952

———■———

"I have to be in charge of myself."

—*PAT AND MIKE*, 1952

"I'm the independent type—

always have been!"

—*SUMMERTIME*, 1955

"I was so selfish. I was a real pig. Always worried about me, me, me."

———■———

"I don't want to be worshipped. I want to be loved . . . I mean really loved!"

—*THE PHILADELPHIA STORY*, 1940

"I'm perfect; everybody knows I'm perfect!"

—*THE RAINMAKER*, 1956

——■——

"Pride, I ran out of pride a long time ago . . . I just want to be a woman . . ."

—*THE RAINMAKER*, 1956

"I want somebody to be glad he found me, the way I'll be glad I found him. I want him to be able to tell me who he is and to tell me who I am too. Because heaven knows I have no idea who I am."

—*THE RAINMAKER*, 1956

■

"All right, all right! I stand accused of generosity."

—*SUDDENLY LAST SUMMER*, 1959

" In my relationships I know I have qualities that are offensive to people—especially men. I'm loud and talkative and I get into subjects that irritate. If I feel things cause a break, I know something has to give. I never think the man is going to give—or anyone else, for that matter—so I do. I just deliberately change. I just shut up—when every atom in me wants to speak up. "

"I ain't sinful, I'm hungry!"

—*SPITFIRE*, 1934

———■———

"I remember walking as a child. It was not customary to say you were fatigued. It was customary to complete the goal of the expedition."

"Now to squash a rumor! I do not have Parkinson's. I inherited my shaking head from my grandfather Hepburn. I discovered that whiskey helps stop the shaking; problem is, it stops the rest of you too! My head just shakes, but I promise you, it ain't gonna fall off!"

On Life

"I love rain. It's lucky, I always think."

"Perhaps I played the fool myself, in choosing to live such a lonely life."

—*MORNING GLORY,* 1933

———■———

"Friendship, if somebody holds out his hand toward you, you've got to reach and take it . . . There are too many people alone, and if you're lucky enough for somebody to want you as a friend, it's an obligation."

—*THE RAINMAKER,* 1956

"I don't care what is written about me, as long as it isn't true."

"If you obey all the rules,
you miss all the fun!"

———■———

"I think everyone is an opportunist
if they have an opportunity."

"There's no harm in a little revenge."

—*LOVE AMONG THE RUINS*, 1975

———■———

"When did an apology ever

mend a harm?"

—*LOVE AMONG THE RUINS*, 1975

"Self-sacrificing women give me melancholia. My mother, who was an angel, always said, 'Please yourself; then at least one person is pleased.'"

"Why slap them on the wrist with a feather when you can belt them over the head with a sledgehammer?"

" Trying to be fascinating is an asinine position to be in. "

———■———

" If you survive long enough, you're revered—rather like an old building. "

"It's life, isn't it? You plow ahead and make a hit. And you plow on and someone passes you. Then someone passes them. Time levels."

"Life's what's important. Walking, houses, family. Birth and pain and joy—and then death. Acting's just waiting for the custard pie. That's all!"

"Enemies are so stimulating."

"I'm very literal-minded. If it's something that nobody can know definitely about, it doesn't bother me. I'll just do the best I can do in this life."

---■---

"I think it's very awkward to be a mild friend. Best to be a very good friend, because all the guards are down and you have total freedom."

"Don't crave work and don't crave idleness either."

———■———

"Women should act the way they are. Their brains are just as good as men's. They could accomplish practically anything a man could accomplish. I mean, they can write, they can paint, they can play tennis so goddamn good. I just hope women don't try to become men. I go mad when they become firemen, and I think of myself in this house if it were burning and women were holding the net."

"Of course women are at a terrible disadvantage in this world. The order of things is practically guaranteed to give them an inferiority complex."

———■———

"I find a woman's point of view much grander and finer than a man's."

"There is seldom a way to explain what are the things that hurt one deeply. They are usually quite foolish. Some little hope or pride—like my singing, for instance—or the size of my eyes."

———■———

"If you don't improve you slip inevitably backward. Or you hammer—hammer—hammer on the same spot. And you become the same old thing doing the same old thing."

"There's a curious lack of humor today . . . I mean, funny to them is a bit boring to me. They laugh at jokes but there's not much wit."

"The thing about life is that you must survive. Life is going to be difficult, and dreadful things will happen. What you do is to move along, get on with it, and be tough. Not in the sense of being mean to others, but tough with yourself and making a deadly effort not to be defeated."

"The terrible thing that is happening today is that people say, 'Oh but I'm so'—well tough titty, you know? You can't be that silly. You have got to face the problems of life."

"... a filthy idea, coming into a private house with a camera ... not in my home."

—*THE PHILADELPHIA STORY*, 1940

"In a world where carpenters get resurrected, anything is possible!"

—*KEEPER OF THE FLAME*, 1942

———■———

"I have many regrets, and I'm sure everyone does. The stupid things you do, you regret if you have any sense, and if you don't regret them, maybe you're stupid."

"Every living being is capable of attack, if sufficiently provoked. Assault lies dormant within us all; it requires only circumstances to set it in violent motion."

—*ADAM'S RIB*, 1949

———■———

"I pray for guidance and blush when I get it."

—*WITHOUT LOVE*, 1945

"Nature is what we are put on this earth to rise above."

—*THE AFRICAN QUEEN*, 1951

———■———

"I never dreamed that any mere experience could be so stimulating."

—*THE AFRICAN QUEEN*, 1951

"Do or die! That's me."

—*PAT AND MIKE,* 1952

———■———

"If there's going to be any trouble, I want my share of it!"

—*PAT AND MIKE,* 1952

" It's the height of bad manners

to eat everything. "

—*THE MADWOMAN OF CHAILLOT,* 1969

"Say something funny.

Make me stop wanting to cry."

—*SUDDENLY LAST SUMMER*, 1959

"Life is hard. After all, it kills you!"

"Life is a thief."

—*SUDDENLY LAST SUMMER*, 1959

On *Love* and **Marriage**

"I don't believe in marriage, it's bloody impractical to love, honor, and obey. If it weren't, you wouldn't have to sign a contract."

"Only really plain people know about love—the very fascinating ones try so hard to create an impression that they soon exhaust their talents!"

———■———

"You don't pick who you fall in love with. There are so few people to love. It's hard for one adult to even like another. Almost impossible!"

"If you want to sacrifice the admiration of many men for the criticism of one, go ahead, get married."

"I mean, I can carry the logs up from the cellar and build a fire. I do all that. But if I were married to someone and I did it and he was sitting reading the paper, I would like him to feel that he's a lazy son of a bitch!"

"Love has nothing to do with what you are expecting to get—only what you are expecting to give—which is everything."

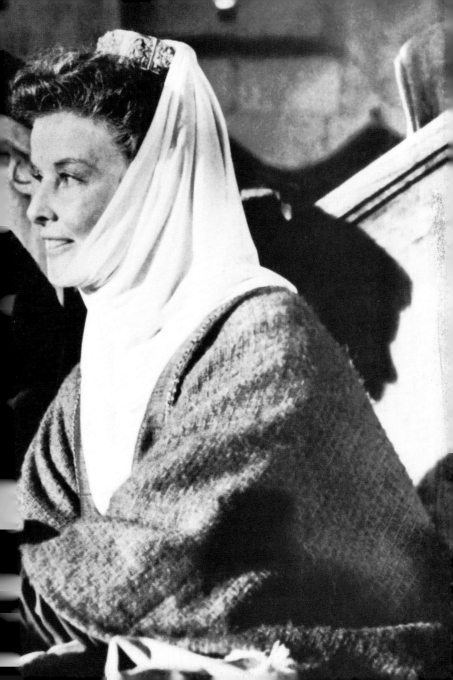

"What in the world would I do with a husband? I have to be totally selfish to live the way I do."

"Well, I'll never marry. I want to be a star, and I don't want to make my husband my victim. And I certainly don't want to make my children my victims."

———■———

"Only when a woman decides not to have children can a woman live like a man. That's what I've done."

"I thought I was fascinating, so I thought, I'm not going to get involved in all that husband and kid business. I married a man, tortured him, used up all his money, drove his automobile and then said good-bye. And he was an angel. Now, I knew it, and I tried to make it up—he's now dead—to him for the enormous generosity of spirit. And I certainly realized that I was a total pig. Now, that's not good, is it? To be a pig?"

———■———

"I'm honest, I'm honest. I face the fact. I missed all the things of being a woman, didn't I? I had no children."

"You see, I loved you for such a long time. Since way this afternoon."

"Do I look the sort of woman who seduces and betrays young boys? As the newspapers have implied?"

—*LOVE AMONG THE RUINS*, 1975

—■—

"You never want love in your life again. I never want it in mine, but our reasons are as different as the sun is from the moon. You don't want it because you've had all the worst. I don't want it because I've had all the best!"

—*WITHOUT LOVE*, 1945

"What does the word 'love' mean? It means total interest. I believe that the reason very few people really fall in love with anyone is that they're not willing to pay the price!"

"Promise you will always let me do what I want to do, or we'll both be terribly unhappy."

—*CHRISTOPHER STRONG*, 1933

"My family wouldn't have permitted Shakespeare himself to call on me, because he was a married man."

—*MORNING GLORY*, 1933

On **Career** and

Acting

"Acting is the perfect idiot's profession."

"Acting is the most minor of gifts and not a very high-class way to earn a living. After all, Shirley Temple could do it at age four."

———■———

"I'm a personality as well as an actress! Show me an actress who isn't a personality and you'll show me a woman who isn't a star."

"The average Hollywood film star's ambition is to be admired by an American, courted by an Italian, married to an Englishman, and have a French boyfriend."

"I can't stand Mary of Scotland. I think she was an ass . . . I thought Elizabeth was absolutely right to have her condemned to death!"

—ON THE MAKING OF *MARY OF SCOTLAND*, 1936

"They can't make me a movie star if I don't want to be one. I've been fired from stage shows five times. Every time it was for trying to uphold one of my personal principles. I was taken back three times; so it proves that I was right at least most of the time."

"I have no idea why I became an actor. I wasn't very bright, so no, not bright, not too intelligent. And I thought I was a good golfer, but sports don't last. I would have loved to have been a tennis champion, but I wasn't that good, so what was I going to do? Persuade someone to marry me?"

———■———

"I thought of being a doctor, and then I thought, well, when I wanted to be a doctor . . . women didn't operate, they didn't do anything. So I thought, well, I can't do that."

" There's a lot to be said for knowing everybody you're working with because it's so terribly embarrassing to have to keep explaining your eccentricities to strangers. "

"So many people see work as such a burden, and that's such a sad thing. They think, 'How wonderful when I retire and stop working forever.' Never realizing that when work ends, a big part of life ends, and that to retire completely is to die."

"All that kept me alive during my childhood were dreams of being a grown-up and a famous actress.**"**

—*LOVE AMONG THE RUINS*, 1975

"I don't give a rat about nudity. But I give an enormous rat when people are disillusioned. It's the style now to show everybody doing everything.**"**

———■———

"I think the style of women is terribly confused . . . look at the parts women play on screen now. Most of them are just poor old things who are tearing off their clothes and rolling around in bed.**"**

"I'm sick and tired of me. I'll get out of me for a while and be someone else."

—*THE RAINMAKER*, 1956

"I'll play any part that appeals to me for twenty dollars."

—*MORNING GLORY*, 1933

"Isn't money a lovely thing!
I hope they don't take it
away from us.**"**

—*THE DESK SET*, 1957

On *Fashion*

"I'm only comfortable in men's clothes."

"I wear my sort of clothes to save me the trouble of deciding which clothes to wear."

———■———

"No! I've never dressed up for any man. If I thought he cared how I looked, I would have thought he was a fool. I really would have."

"Now, I know I dress like a freak—I think I enjoy it. I can understand why young people dress like freaks. Because, my God, that trip, until you go down the drain, is very short. I think people who survive are the people who are not such insane egomaniacs that they have to put their mark on everything."

———■———

"I may look odd walking across Claridge's lobby, but I'm the height of chic in the jungle!"

"I think the short skirt is really fundamentally hideous."

———■———

"The thing that drove me out of skirts was the stocking situation. Stockings are just hopeless. Tights? Tights are so hot—oh, can't stand them! That's why I've always worn pants . . . that way you can always go barefoot!"

"I think some of the style happened naturally—the pants came because I didn't like stockings and I like low heels. I was comfortable in bigger clothes. I like the look of a double-sized sleeve. I thought my neck was too scrawny, so I covered it up with a turtleneck. I have a little face, and I didn't want a great big collar with a little face coming out of it, so I had little collars. Practical."

"I think most girls have a white dress they remember, or are remembered in."

—*WITHOUT LOVE*, 1945

"My father was like me. He had no clothes at all! He had a change of clothes, and he had evening clothes, and he had tails. That's it! They fit in one small cupboard. And the theory was sort of Scottish, you know. You had two pairs of shoes. One if the other was wet—and you had a pair of sneakers and you had a pair of pumps."

On Confidence

"I'm the dessert. The ice cream with whipped cream and cake!"

"As one goes through life, one learns that if you don't paddle your own canoe, you don't move!"

———■———

"I was never a victim of the times I lived in. In fact, I was a success because of the times I lived in. My style of personality became the style. I was sort of the new woman at a very early point."

"I just don't like to be half-good. It drives me insane. And I'm willing to do anything to try to be really good. I'm very aware when I'm very good—and I like to be very, very good. I think perfection is the only standard for people who are stars."

———■———

"I could have accomplished three times what I've accomplished. I haven't realized my full potential. It's disgusting."

"From defeat, I learned you have to know a little bit what you are doing and you are the only person who is to blame in your life, really. You can't move on saying, 'Well, I don't want to go this way. I'm going this way because you're pushing me.' Don't do that. There's only one person to blame, and that is you."

"I believe you put the toughness on to save your skin . . . I know a little about that . . . quite a lot!"

"I won't be a girl. I won't be weak and I won't be silly. I'll be a boy! Rough and hard! I won't care what I'll do."

—*SYLVIA SCARLETT*, 1936

———■———

"A boy sows a wild oat or two, the world winks. A girl does the same—scandal."

—*ADAM'S RIB*, 1949

"I like to feel cold; it makes me feel strong."

—*MORNING GLORY*, 1933

———■———

"If you don't understand *Hamlet* then you may be able to understand something else! Though I doubt it by the look of you!"

—*MORNING GLORY*, 1933

"I like hyphens;
   they inspire confidence!"

—*LOVE AMONG THE RUINS*, 1975

On
Spencer
Tracy

"When I met Spencer I discovered myself."

"I loved Spencer Tracy. This was not easy for me because I was definitely a me, me person."

"On screen I think Spencer and I are the perfect American couple—the ideal American man is certainly Spencer Tracy. Sports-loving, man's man, strong-looking, big sort of head, boar neck, and so forth. A man. And I think I represent a woman. I needle him, and if he put a big paw out and put it on my head, he could squash me. And I think that this is the real romantic ideal picture of the male and female in this country."

"He had me; I didn't necessarily have him."

"Much of what I know about acting I learned from Spencer Tracy . . . a sturdy oak buffeted by the wind—a throwback to an age of heroism . . . that vanishing American, the self-made man. He was what we imagined our grandfathers to be."

———■———

"Spencer was a real baked potato . . . a great actor. Simple. Never overdone. Unguarded. He could make you laugh. He could make you cry."

"I was very careful that we were not gossiped about. The press were very nice to us, when they could have been hurtful."

———■———

"In the last years of Spencer's life I didn't act so much . . . He was my good, good friend and that seemed wonderful to me to be useful."

On Other
Leading Men

ADOLPHE MENJOU

"Wisecracking, witty—a flag-waving super patriot who invested his American dollars in Canadian bonds and had a thing for communists."

HENRY FONDA

"Henry Fonda's not one to make new friends and neither am I, but we got along okay. He has his own world. He likes to fish, I like to walk through the woods alone . . . He doesn't waste time. No small talk. And I hate to have idiotic conversations. We found we could work together just like that—and we really did."

HUMPHREY BOGART

"He was a real man—nothing feminine about him. He knew he was a natural aristocrat—better than anybody."

JOHN WAYNE

"From head to toe he is all of a piece. Big head. Wild blue eyes. Sandy hair. Rugged skin—lined by living, and fun and character. Not just by rotting away. A nose not too big, not too small. Good teeth. A face alive with humor. Good humor, I should say, and sharp wit. Dangerous when roused . . . He's sweet, gentle, and he's a monster."

MONTGOMERY CLIFT

"I thought he was weak—simpatico but weak."

TO FELLINI

"Oh, Federico, your early movies were just fine, straightforward, realistic. But then just like crazy Picasso, you've gone berserk. I mean, that absurd *Juliet of the Spirits*? What on earth was all that about?"

On **Aging**

Gracefully

"Wonderful things can happen,
no matter how old you are!"

"The people who are alive are the ones that interest me. I'm not particularly interested in the next world, because I have no control over it!"

———■———

"Someone once asked me, who was about my age, 'How are you?' 'Fine, if you don't ask for details.'"

"When people have known you all their lives, it puts you in the queer position of being everybody's grandma. Then there are people who come up to me on the street, throw their arms around me, and then say, 'It's you—Audrey Hepburn."

———■———

"You have never done it all, until you can't do it."

"Isn't it nice of the drugstore to keep me alive."

—*SUDDENLY LAST SUMMER*, 1959

—■—

"There comes a time in your life when people get very sweet to you. I don't mind people being very sweet; I'm getting rather sweet back to them. But I'm a madly irritating person and I irritated them for years. Anything definite is irritating— and stimulating. I think they're beginning to think that I'm not going to be around much longer. And what do you know— they'll miss me, like an old monument. Like the Flatiron Building."

"In time, of course, the rage passes, and one is able to face one's loss and accept it."

—*LOVE AMONG THE RUINS*, 1975

———■———

"It seems to me that we spend our lives just missing people; you look at someone, and you know they're tortured. Then they die, and you think, 'Why didn't I say that?'"

"We're at the far edge of middle age, that's all."

—*ON GOLDEN POND*, 1981

"It's a bore—**B-O-R-E**—when you find out you've begun to rot."

On **Death**

"Die and leave everything in a mess!
That's what I intend to do."

"I welcome death. In death there are no interviews!"

Filmography

A Bill of Divorcement (1932)

Christopher Strong (1933)

Morning Glory (1933)

Little Women (1933)

Spitfire (1934)

The Little Minister (1934)

Break of Hearts (1935)

Alice Adams (1935)

Sylvia Scarlett (1936)

Mary of Scotland (1936)

A Woman Rebels (1936)

Quality Street (1937)

Stage Door (1937)

Bringing Up Baby (1938)

Holiday (1938)

The Philadelphia Story (1940)

Woman of the Year (1942)

Keeper of the Flame (1942)

Dragon Seed (1944)

Without Love (1945)

Undercurrent (1946)

The Sea of Grass (1947)

Song of Love (1947)

State of the Union (1948)

Adam's Rib (1949)

The African Queen (1951)

Pat and Mike (1952)

Summertime (1955)

The Rainmaker (1956)

The Iron Petticoat (1956)

The Desk Set (1957)

Suddenly Last Summer (1959)

Long Day's Journey Into Night
   (1962)

Guess Who's Coming to Dinner
   (1967)

The Lion in Winter (1968)

The Madwoman of Chaillot
   (1969)

The Trojan Women (1971)

A Delicate Balance (1973)

The Glass Menagerie (1973)

Love Among the Ruins (1975)

Rooster Cogburn (1975)

Oily Oily Oxen Free (1978)

The Corn Is Green (1979)

On Golden Pond (1981)

Grace Quigley (1985)

Mrs. Delafield Wants to Marry
   (1986)

Laura Lansing Slept Here
   (1988)

The Man Upstairs (1992)

This Can't Be Love (1994)

One Christmas (1994)

Love Affair (1994)

Acknowledgments

This tribute to the great Katharine Hepburn would not have been possible without Executive Editor Maureen O'Brien, who had the brilliant idea of preserving Kate's memorable lines, and worked so hard to get it done. And thanks to Rakia Clark for all her help. Special thanks are also due to the following news organizations, media outlets, and people whose work or input helped in one way or another. Tom Gilbert at Associated Press, Wide World Photos. Author Anne Edwards. Wendy Wasserstein. Cindy Adams, the *New York Post.* Candace Trunzo, American Media. The archives of *People* magazine, *World Telegraph and Sun,* the *New York Times,* the *Washington Post, Chicago Sun-Times, The Saturday Evening Post,* the *Los Angeles Times, New World Telegram, Time* magazine, *Los Angeles* magazine, *Entertainment Tonight,* Paramount Television. The BBC, ABC, CBS. Kate's Web ring. Knopf. Random House. Wendy Buck, Kim Small, Virgin Atlantic Airways. Michaela Parris Lord, Mimi Strong, and Frederick Crimp. Lottie Lherhoff. And to my dearest sisters M. Ancy, M. Dominga, and M. Sabita. And finally to my dear friend the Reverend Halligan.

Source Notes

The Philadelphia Story, 1940

ON SELF 1

New York Daily News, September 11, 1982
Me, Random House, 1991
Katharine Hepburn webring
World Telegram and Sun, September 27, 1962
World Telegram and Sun, September 27, 1962
Katharine Hepburn webring
Katharine Hepburn webring
ABC *Primetime Live*, October 18, 1990
CBS, December 3, 1990
New York Times, November 15, 1981
Chicago Sun-Times
Louella Parsons, April 14, 1957
Saturday Evening Post
New York *Daily News*, June 30, 2003
Pat and Mike, 1932
Pat and Mike, 1932
Summertime, 1955
Los Angeles Times, September 1, 1991
The Philadelphia Story, 1940
The Rainmaker, 1956
The Rainmaker, 1956
The Rainmaker, 1956
Suddenly Last Summer, 1959
A Remarkable Woman, Anne Edwards

Spitfire, 1934
www.geocities.com/Paris/Arc/4941/qxhepburn.html
The Internet Movie Database. IMDb

ON LIFE 25

The Making of The African Queen, Knopf, 1987
Morning Glory, 1933
The Rainmaker, 1956
Wendy Wasserstein article
Brainymedia.com
New York Daily News, September 1, 1991
Love Among the Ruins, 1975
Love Among the Ruins, 1975
Creativequotes.com
Associated Press biography number 4648
ABC News, October, 1990
Katharine Hepburn Webring
Womanshistory.About.com
Womanshistory.About.com
Womanshistory.About.com
Womanshistory.About.com
People magazine, March 14, 1988
Los Angeles Magazine, March 1997
Chicago Sun-Times
Los Angeles Times, September 1, 1991
New World Telegram, September 27, 1962

The Internet Movie Database. IMDb
Me, Random House, 1991
Katharine Hepburn webring
New York Daily News, June 30, 2003
ABC News, October 18, 1990
The Philadelphia Story, 1940
Keeper of the Flame, 1942
Womanshistory.About.com
Adam's Rib, 1949
Without Love, 1945
The African Queen, 1951
The African Queen, 1951
Pat and Mike, 1952
Pat and Mike, 1952
The Madwoman of Chaillot, 1969
Suddenly Last Summer, 1959
Womanshistory.About.com
Suddenly Last Summer, 1959

ON LOVE AND MARRIAGE   57

Brainymedia.com
Brainymedia.com
Time magazine, June 29, 1992
Brainymedia.com
People magazine, November 5, 1990
Me, Random House, 1991
New York Daily News, September 9,
    1982
A Remarkable Woman, Anne Edwards
Brainymedia.com
CBS, September 6, 1991
ABC News, October, 1990
Break of Hearts, 1935
Love Among the Ruins, 1975
Without Love, 1945
20/20, September 6, 1991
Christopher Strong, 1933
Morning Glory, 1933

ON CAREER AND ACTING   77

Katharine Hepburn Webring
BBC

famouscreativequotes.com
New York Newsday, September 1, 1991
The Internet Movie Database. IMDb
New York Daily News, June 30, 2003
New York Daily News, December 13,
    1932
20/20, September 6, 1991
CBS, December 3, 1990
A Remarkable Woman, Anne Edwards
New York World Telegram, September
    21, 1962
Love Among the Ruins, 1975
Los Angeles Magazine, March 1997
New York Times, November 15, 1981
The Rainmaker, 1956
Morning Glory, 1933
The Desk Set, 1957

ON FASHION   95

New York Daily News, November 5,
    1967
The Internet Movie Database. IMDb
Washington Post, March 9, 1986
Los Angeles Magazine, March 1997
The Making of The African Queen,
    Knopf, 1987
Washington Post, March 9, 1980
New York Times, November 15, 1981
Washington Post, March 9, 1980
Without Love, 1945
Washington Post, March 9, 1980

ON CONFIDENCE   107

New York Daily News, November 5,
    1967
famouscreativewomen.com
Los Angeles Times, September 1,
    1991
A Remarkable Woman, Anne Edwards
Associated Press biography number
    4648
20/20, September 6, 1991

The Philadelphia Story, 1940
Sylvia Scarlett, 1936
Adam's Rib, 1949
Morning Glory, 1933
Morning Glory, 1933
Love Among the Ruins, 1975

ON SPENCER TRACY   119

Entertainment Tonight, June 30, 2003
Me, Random House, 1991
Me, Random House, 1991
Glenn Plaskin, New York *Daily News*,
   1991
Entertainment Tonight, June 30, 2003
New York *Daily News*, June 30, 2003
Glenn Plaskin, New York *Daily News*,
   1991
Entertainment Tonight, June 30, 2003
Entertainment Tonight, June 30, 2003

ON OTHER LEADING MEN   129

New York *Daily News*, June 30, 2003
New York *Daily News*, June 30, 2003

New York *Daily News*, June 30, 2003
New York *Daily News*, June 30, 2003
New York *Daily News*, June 30, 2003
Shattered Love: A Memoir, Richard
   Chamberlain

ON AGING GRACEFULLY   139

Los Angeles Times, March 29, 1986
New York Times, March 9, 1988
Brainymedia.com
People magazine, March 14, 1988
Los Angeles Times, March 29, 1986
Suddenly Last Summer, 1959
Associated Press biography number
   4648
Love Among the Ruins, 1975
People magazine, March 14, 1988
On Golden Pond, 1981

ON DEATH   148

The Internet Movie Database. IMDb
Brainymedia.com
New York *Newsday*, September 1, 1991